SCIENCE

UNDERSTANDING YOUR ENVIRONMENT

GEORGE G. MALLINSON
Distinguished Professor
of Science Education
Western Michigan University

JACQUELINE B. MALLINSON
Associate Professor of Science
Western Michigan University

DOUGLAS G. BROWN
Teacher at the Individualized Learning Center
Sioux City, Iowa, Community Schools

JOHN KNAPP II
Associate Professor of Science Education
State University of New York—Oswego

WILLIAM L. SMALLWOOD
Teacher and Former Science Coordinator
Mountain Home, Idaho, Public Schools

SILVER, BURDETT & GINN INC.
LEXINGTON, MA • MORRISTOWN, NJ
Atlanta, GA • Cincinnati, OH • Dallas, TX • Menlo Park, CA • Northfield, IL

SCIENCE

UNDERSTANDING YOUR ENVIRONMENT

THE SILVER BURDETT ELEMENTARY SCIENCE PROGRAM K-6

PUPIL'S BOOKS AND TEACHERS' EDITIONS
LEVELS ONE THROUGH SIX

RECORD BOOKS IN SPIRIT-MASTER FORM
LEVELS THREE THROUGH SIX

AUTHORS:
GEORGE G. MALLINSON
JACQUELINE B. MALLINSON
DOUGLAS G. BROWN
WILLIAM L. SMALLWOOD
JOHN KNAPP II

Critic Readers
Dr. Jean Adenika
University of California
Irvine, California

Richard Codispoti
Director, Science Education
Cleveland Public Schools
Cleveland, Ohio

Luis Antonio Cordova
Colegio Our Lady of Pilar
Hato Rey, Puerto Rico

Sister Marie Savickas, C.S.A.
Universty of Minnesota
Morris, Minnesota

Jack R. Warren
Science Coordinator
Clayton County Schools
Jonesboro, Georgia

Individualized Extension Activities
Enrichment and Evaluative Materials (pupil
activity sheets on spirit masters)
for Grades 1 and 2
Teachers' Guides

Science Labs
Levels 1–6

Sound Filmstrips
60 filmstrips and cassettes for Levels 1–6

Beginner Series in Science
Multimedia Learning Activity Units with
sound filmstrips

Pictures That Teach–Science
28 charts and Teacher's Manual

Environment Education Picture Packet
24 pictures and Teacher's Manual

ISBN 0-382-04870-9

CONTENTS

1

WATER ON THE EARTH

Water is found everywhere on the earth.

Water is in the oceans.

Water is in rivers and lakes.

Water is in the ground.

Water is found in the air.

Where is most of the earth's water?

Could you drink this water?

Why?

Water in lakes and rivers is fresh water.

Fresh water is not too salty to drink.

These boys are near the ocean.

Where is the water coming from?

Where does your drinking water come from?

Have you ever eaten any of these?

What are they?

All these foods came from animals.

The animals lived in water.

ACTIVITY

These are the animals the foods came from.
Do they live in fresh water, or salt water?
Find out.

Many plants and animals live in water.

More plants live in the ocean than on the land.

Learn more about water plants.

Get two freshwater aquarium plants.

Grow one in fresh water.

Grow one in salt water.

What happens?

ACTIVITY

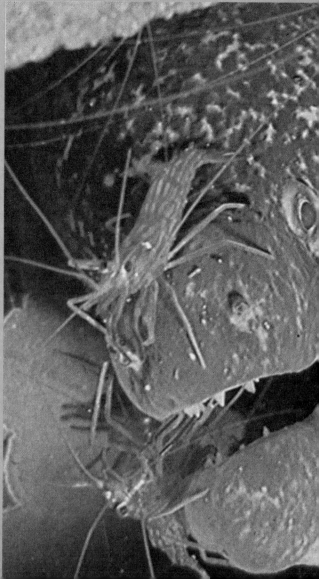

We don't know much about the oceans.
But we are studying them.
Some day much of our food may come from oceans.

Most of the water on the earth is a liquid.

In some places it is a solid.

Where do you see solid water here?

Water can also be a gas.

It is called water vapor.

You cannot see water vapor.

Water can be a liquid.

It can also be a solid or a gas.

What do you call solid water?

ACTIVITY

What do you call water that is a gas?

Try this.

Try to change the liquid back to a solid.

This shows how water changes.
Water in the lake changes to water
vapor.
The water vapor goes into the air.
Can you see the water vapor
in the air?
The water vapor changes again if
the air is cooled.
It changes back to little drops
of liquid.
Sometimes the little drops get bigger.
The bigger drops form rain.
Rain falls to the earth.
Water vapor may travel far before
it forms drops.
But everywhere water is always
changing.

Sun

Clouds

Water vapor

clouds
move

rain

water

You have learned that water can be changed.

But water can also change things.

Get some things like these.

Put them in water.

Do they change?

Make a chart like this one.

Gelatin dessert	
Sugar cubes	
Marbles	
Bread	
Candy mint	
Macaroni	

Does water change these things?
Write Yes or No.

What has water changed here?
How did it change the earth?
How long do you think it took?

ACTIVITY

Water can be used in many ways.
Water changes most solids.

Get different kinds of solid matter.
Put some of each solid into water.
What happens?

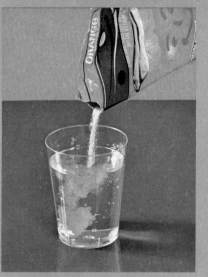

Do all solids change the same way in water?

How do you know a solid changes?

Make a list of solids that change.

Mix some salt in water.

Put the salt water in a warm place.

Let it stand for a day or two.

Tell what happens.

Where does the water go?

How can you make this happen faster?

This was once a pond.
What happened to the water?
Where did it go?
Where else have you seen this happen?

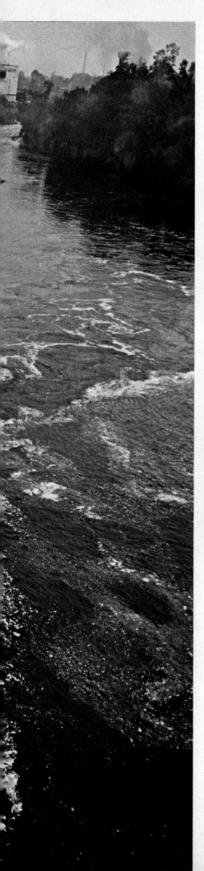

Sometimes people change water.
How has water been changed here?
Are these changes good, or bad?
Why?
How can we stop these changes?

We need clean water for many reasons.

One reason is to help plants and animals.

Plants need water to make food.

Animals need water to carry food through their bodies.

How do you use water?

29

CHECKUP

1. Where is water found?
2. Find liquid and solid water in the pictures.
3. How can water be changed?
4. How does water change the earth?
5. What can live in water?
6. Name some things that change in water.
7. Why must we take care of our water?
8. How can you help keep water clean?

WHAT IS AIR?

Air is all around you.

But what is air?

Can you see it?

Can you feel it?

How do you know it is there?

Go outside on a clear day.

How do you know there is air around you?

Who is winning this race?

Why?

What does this show about air?

Try this yourself.

ACTIVITY

What are these children making?
What would you need to make one?
Try to do it.
What does this show about air?

What is happening here?
How does air help?
How do you use air?

What is in the big balloon?

Which balloon weighs more?

How can you tell?

What do these pictures show
about air?
Try one of these activities.
What other ways will show this?

ACTIVITY

This activity will show you more about air.
Put some water in a large dish.
Push a dry cloth into a glass.

Turn the glass upside down in the water.
Does water go into the glass?
How do you know?

What does this show about air?

Sometimes we fill things with air.
What happens if we put in too much air?

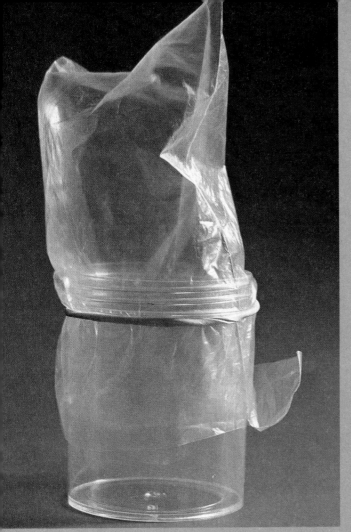

Put a plastic bag over a jar.
Try to push the bag into the jar.
Can you do it?

Now put the bag inside
   the jar.
Try to pull it out.
Can you do it?
What do these activities show
   about air?

Air pushes up and it pushes down.
Air pushes on the sides of things.

Fill a glass with water.

Put a card over the top of the glass.

ACTIVITY

Turn the glass over.

Take your hand off the card.

What happens? Why?

All living things need air.

Where do fish get air?

Where do these plants get air?

What happens if fish are taken out of water?

Could you live under water?

You take air into your lungs.

Frogs have lungs, too.

Frogs also take in air through their skin.

What do these pictures show about air?
Is the air like this where you live?
Where do you think the pictures were taken?
Is this air good for living things?

49

How are these pictures different?
Where do you think they were taken?
Where is air probably cleaner?
Why?

	Clean	Dirty
Near school		
Near home		
Downtown		
In the park		
Near factory		

These things help make air dirty.

Tell about each one.

Look around your city or town.

What can be done to make air clean?

ACTIVITY

1. Where is air found?
2. How do you know air is all around you?
3. Which pictures show that air takes up space?
4. How do you know that air has weight?
5. Which picture shows that air pushes?
   Where is it pushing?
6. Where would you find clean air?
7. Where would you find dirty air?
8. What things make air dirty?

YOU AND THE WEATHER

What is the weather like in this picture?

Why is weather important to people?

Why do you need to know about weather?

There are many kinds of weather.
What is the weather like here?
What kinds of weather have you seen?
What kinds of weather do you have?

Keep a record of the weather where you live.

Do this every day for two weeks.

What does your record show about weather?

Here are three places on the earth.
What is the weather like in each place?
What is the weather like where you live?

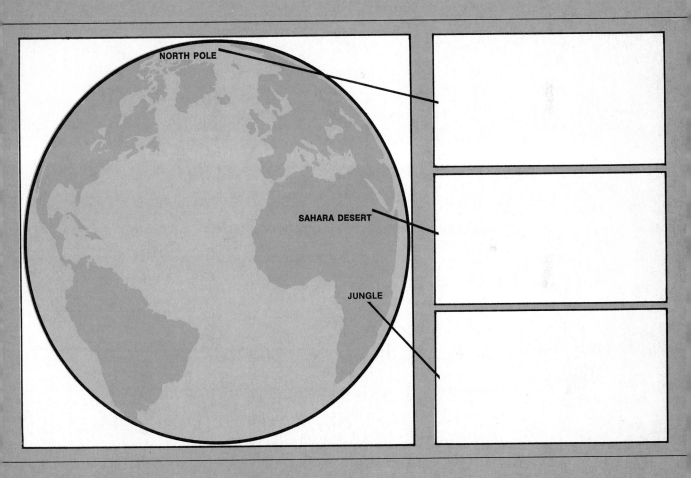

NORTH POLE

SAHARA DESERT

JUNGLE

Find some weather pictures.

Where do you think they were taken?

Draw a globe like this one.

Paste your pictures where they belong on the globe.

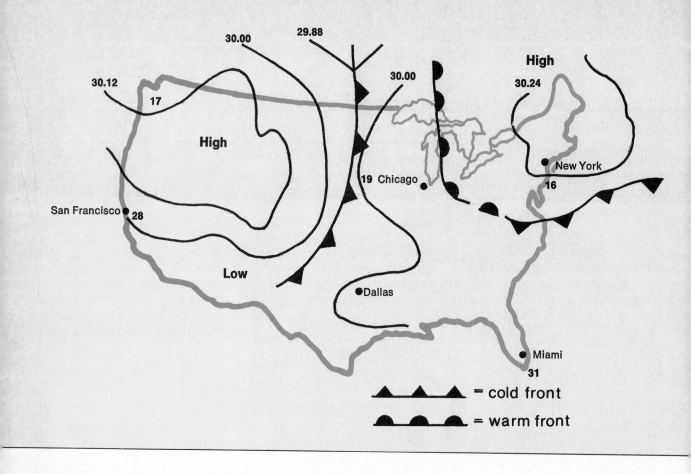

Some people study the weather.

They put the information on a map.

The map helps them tell what the weather will be.

Can you name the things in these pictures?

What do they measure?

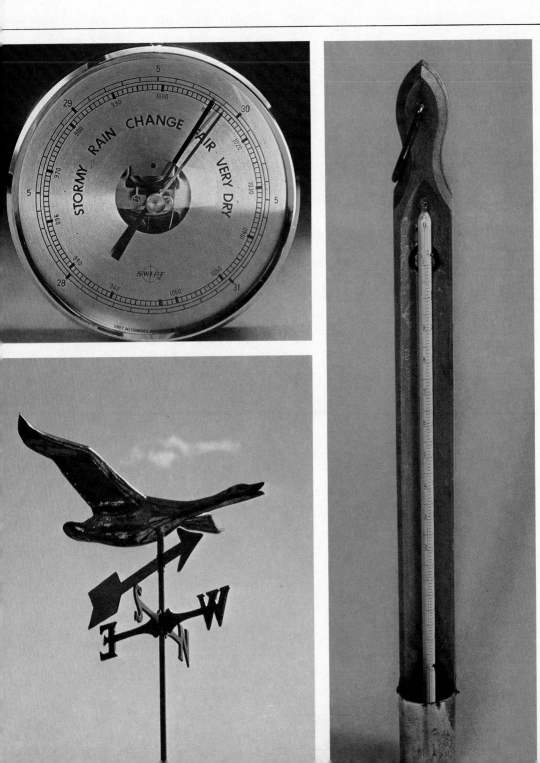

Some days it is cool when you go to school.
But it may be warm when you go home.

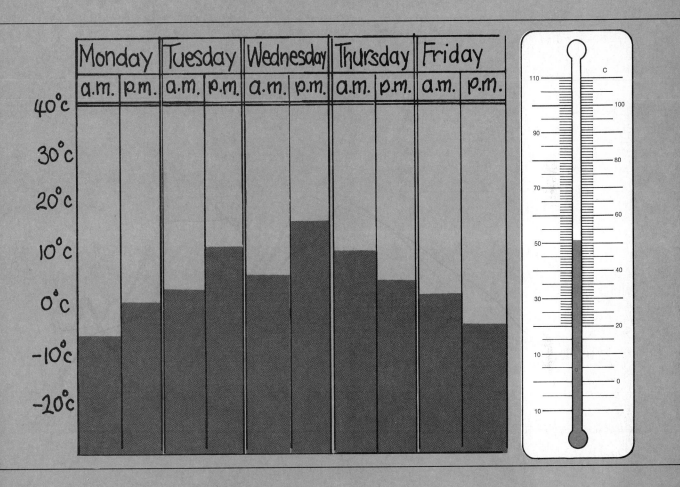

A thermometer tells how hot or cold it is.

Learn to use a thermometer.

Make a chart like this one.

Measure the temperature at the same time each morning.

Do the same each afternoon.

Put your readings on the chart.

Color in the temperature.

Some places get much rain.
Other places get very little.
How much rain falls where you live?
Is there more rain at different times of the year?
What places get a lot of rain?
What places get very little rain?

ACTIVITY

Make one of these.

Use it to measure rainfall.

Keep a record of the rainfall.

Wind comes with a change in weather.

Make one of these.

What does it tell about weather?

Your activities change when the weather changes.
What do you do in different kinds of weather?
What clothes do you wear in different kinds of weather?
What kind of weather do you like best?

Find pictures showing people
in different kinds of weather.
What are they doing?
What are they wearing?

ACTIVITY

Some animals migrate.
This means they move from one place to another.
Usually they migrate when the weather changes.
They do this to find food.

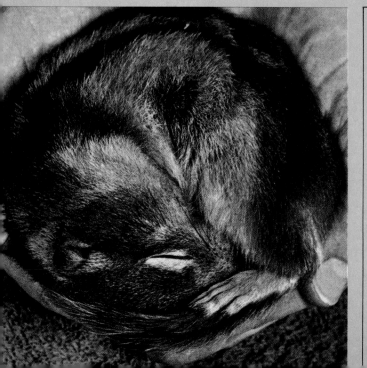

Some animals hibernate in
winter.
Animals that hibernate go
into a kind of winter sleep.
Some of them move about
from time to time.
How can they sleep most of
the winter without food?

Plants cannot migrate or hibernate.

How do plants change when the weather changes?

ACTIVITY

Find pictures of other animals that migrate.

Find pictures of other animals that hibernate.

Find pictures showing how plants change
with the weather.

CHECKUP

1. What kinds of weather do you have?
2. What other kinds of weather are there? Where?
3. Name places where the weather is different from yours.
4. How does your life change when the weather changes?
5. How do some animals change when the weather changes?
6. What happens to plants when the weather changes?
7. What helps us find out about the weather?

ANIMALS AND MORE ANIMALS

There are many kinds of animals on the earth.
There are so many that you cannot count them.
Some animals are very large.
Some are so small that you cannot see them.
How many kinds of animals can you name?
What are these animals called?

Animals live almost everywhere on the earth.
Some live where it is hot.
Some live where it is cold.
What kinds of places do you see here?
What kinds of animals might live here?
What are desert animals like?
How are they different from water animals?

Find pictures of other places.
Draw pictures of animals that
might live there.

ACTIVITY

Make a place for an animal to live in.

A snail jar is easy to make.

Find out what snails need to stay alive.

What will you need to make a snail jar?

Watch the snails every day.

Find out all you can about snails.

Make a list of what they eat.

Tell how they move.

How does a snail use its shell?

Animals have different body coverings.
Some animals are covered with fur.
Some animals are covered with scales.
What kinds of body coverings do you see here?

ACTIVITY

Find pictures of animals with other kinds of body coverings.

Different animals have bodies of different shapes.
Tell about the bodies of these animals.

Think about how animals move.
Think about how animals get food.
Think about how they protect themselves.
How do body shapes help in these things?

You know that all living things need food.

Their bodies need the energy from food.

Animals get food in many different ways.

How does this animal get its food?

How do other animals get their food?

Animals also need water.

Where do animals get their water?

How do you know animals need air?

ACTIVITY

Look at the animals carefully.

How are they alike?

How are they different?

What parts of their bodies help them get food?

What foods do they eat?

Find pictures of other animals.

What foods do they eat?

How do they get their food?

Animals use plants and other animals for food.
Smaller animals are eaten by larger animals.
What is happening in these pictures?
What other animals will these animals eat?
This is called a food web.

These children are showing a food web.
Look at how they are doing it.
You can make a picture of a food web, too.
Plan how you will do it.
Why is this called a food web?

Animals move in different ways.
How do these animals move?
How do other animals move?
What animals move very fast?
What animals move very slowly?
What parts of their bodies help them move?

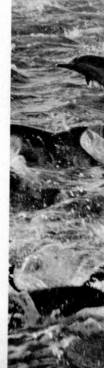

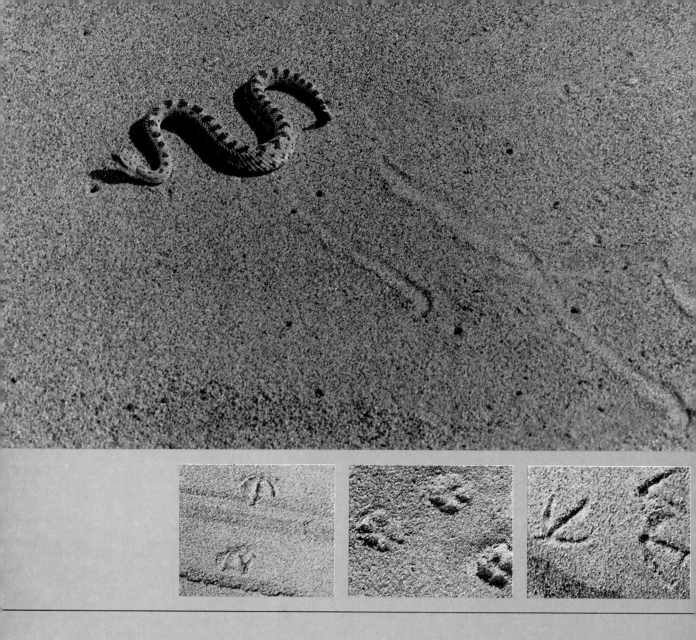

Sometimes animals leave tracks when they move.
You can find out about an animal from its tracks.
What can you tell from these animal tracks?

You can make a mold of an animal track.
What do you think you will need?

ACTIVITY

Many animals have soft bodies.

Where do animals with soft bodies live?

Some animals have a hard covering over a soft body.

Name some animals like that.

Find out where those animals live.

Find pictures of animals with hard body coverings.

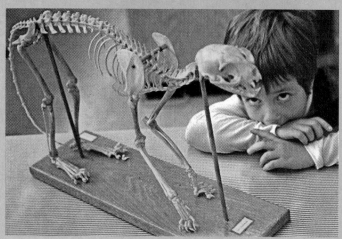

Some animals have a soft body outside.
But they have bones inside their bodies.
Why do some animals need bones?
Why do you need bones?
Name some animals that have bones.

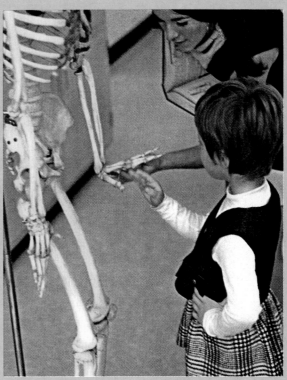

Find pictures of other animals.
Which ones have bones?
Which ones do not have bones?
Make a chart with your pictures.
How could you group your pictures?

1. Tell about the different kinds of places where animals live.
2. What kinds of body coverings do animals have?
3. Name an animal. What does it eat? Tell how it gets its food.
4. Name some animals. Tell how they move.
5. What is a food web?
6. Name some animals that have bones.
7. Name some animals that do not have bones.
8. Why do some animals need bones?

CHECKUP

WHAT IS A MAGNET?

Almost everyone has seen a magnet.

There are many kinds of magnets.

Some magnets are made by people.

Some magnets are rocks from the ground.

Tell about the magnets in this picture.

Magnets are used in many ways.

Some toys have magnets in them.

Get a magnet and see what it can do.

A magnet attracts things.
Will it attract everything?
Try it.

Find some of these things.

Touch each one with a magnet.

Touch some other things with a magnet.

What things will your magnet attract?

What are those things made of?

These children are using magnets.
How are they moving their boats?
What are the boats made of?
Do magnets attract through some things?
How do you know?
Try to find out.

What is the girl doing?

Try to get a clip out of a glass.

Do not touch the clip.

Will a clip come out of a can this way?

Try it and find out.

ACTIVITY

Some magnets are
  very strong.
Some magnets are
  not so strong.
Find the strongest magnet
  in your class.
How can you tell
  which is strongest?

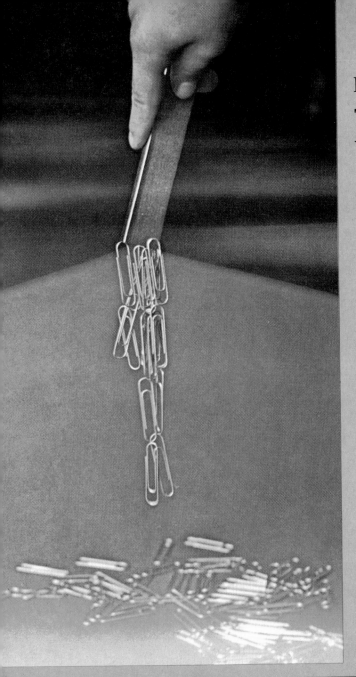

Put a magnet in a pile of clips.
Then lift the magnet.
Where are most of the clips
  on the magnet?
What parts of the magnet are
  the strongest?
These parts are called the poles.
A magnet has two poles.
Find the poles on your magnet.
Where are the poles of these
  magnets?

ACTIVITY

Put the ends of two magnets together.

What do you feel and see?

Now turn one of the magnets around.

Put those two ends together.

What do you feel and see?

Are the poles of a magnet the same?

Are the ends of your magnet marked **N** and **S**?

The **N** means the north pole of the magnet.

The **S** means the south pole of the magnet.

Put two north poles together.

Put two south poles together.

Put a north pole and a south pole together.

What did you find out?

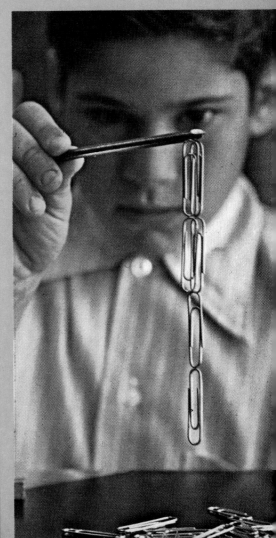

Make a magnet.
Get a new iron nail.
Touch it to some clips.
What happens?

Pull the nail across a strong magnet.
Do this many times in the same way.
Now touch the nail to the clips.
What happens?
How strong is your new magnet?
Who made the strongest magnet?
How can you tell?

CHECKUP

1. What things do magnets attract?
2. What parts of magnets are the strongest?
3. Through what things will magnets attract?
4. Find the poles of the magnets in the pictures.
   What are the poles called?

5. Put the north or south poles of two magnets together.
   What happens?
6. Put the north and south poles together.
   What happens?
7. What are some ways magnets are used?

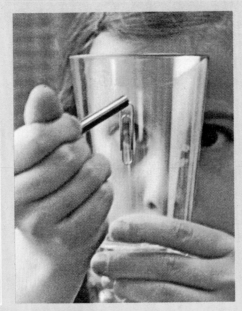

6

LEARNING ABOUT ELECTRICITY

Sometimes your hair makes a noise
   when you comb it.
That noise is made by electricity.
It is static electricity.
Static electricity collects on things.
Then it jumps to other things.
Rub your feet on a rug.
Then touch a doorknob.
What happens?
Where do you see electricity here?

ACTIVITY

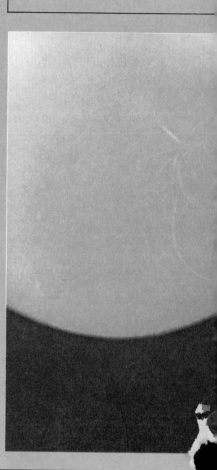

You can make static electricity.
You can do many things with it.
Try these activities.

What do you see when you do these things?
What else can you do with static electricity?

Electricity is used in this lamp.
But it is not static electricity.
Static electricity collects on things.
Then it jumps to other things.
The electricity here moves along wires.
Where do you think it comes from?
Try the next activity.
Find out how this electricity moves.

You can find out how electricity moves.

Get a battery like this one.

You will also need a bulb and a wire.

The battery makes the electricity.

You must move the electricity through the bulb.

Use the wire to make a path for the electricity.

How can you make the bulb light?

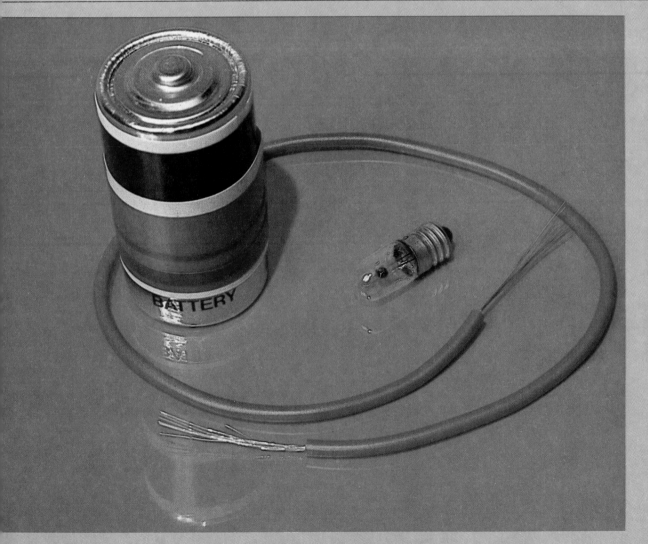

Did you make the bulb light?
Did you do it like this?
This kind of electricity is current electricity.
Current electricity moves along a path.
What makes the path here?

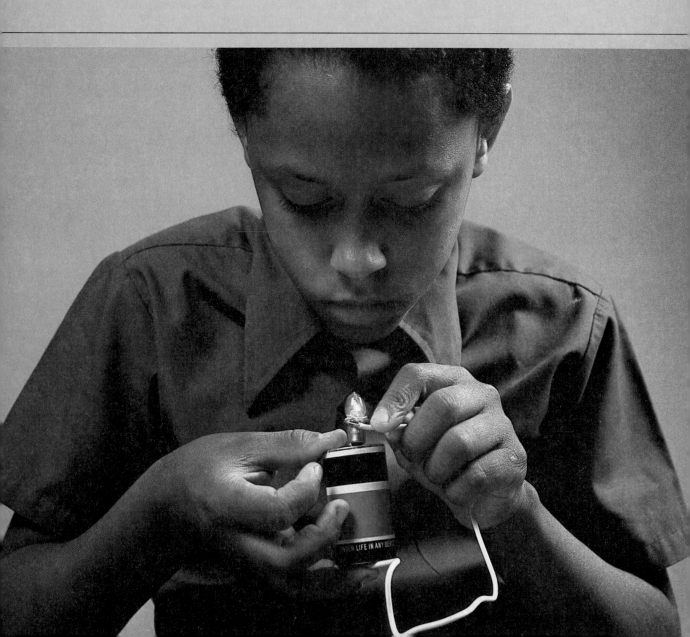

This shows how current electricity moves through a lamp.
How does it move through the flashlight?
Trace both paths.

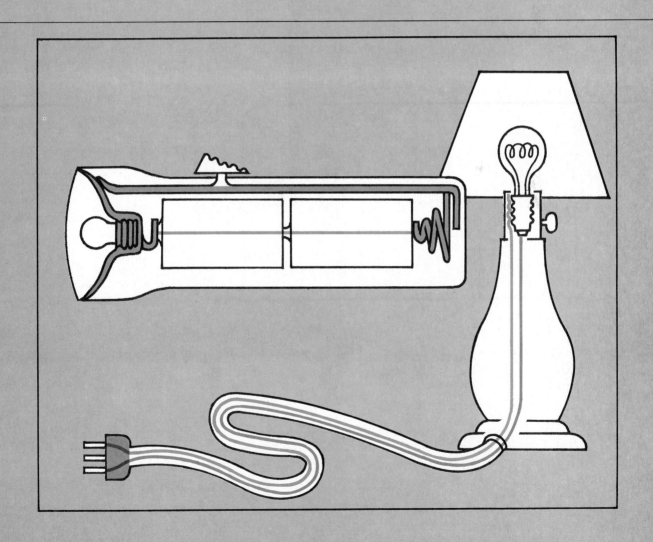

You have learned how to move electricity.

You know it moves along a path.

But can you stop electricity?

How can you break the path?

You can use a switch.

Put a switch in the path.

ACTIVITY

Close the switch.

Does the bulb light?

How can you stop the electricity?

How can you make it move again?

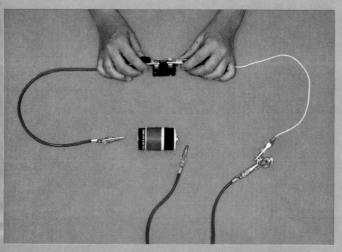

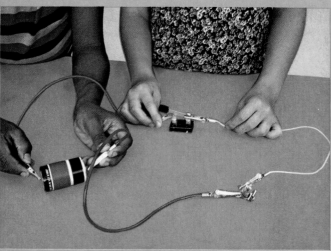

121

You made a magnet
   with a nail.
How did you do it?
Now you can make a magnet
   with electricity.
Touch a new nail to some
   clips.
What happens?

ACTIVITY

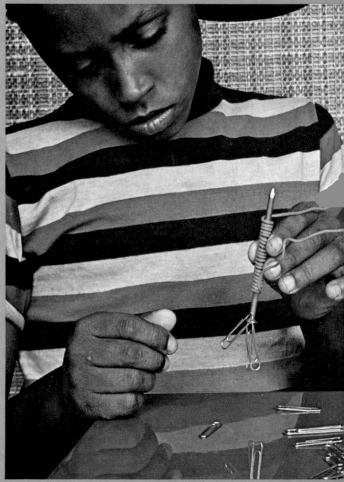

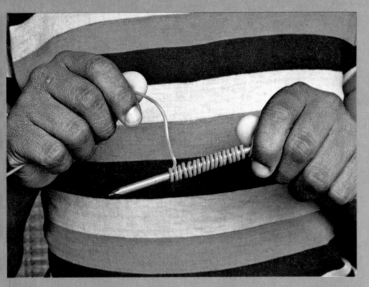

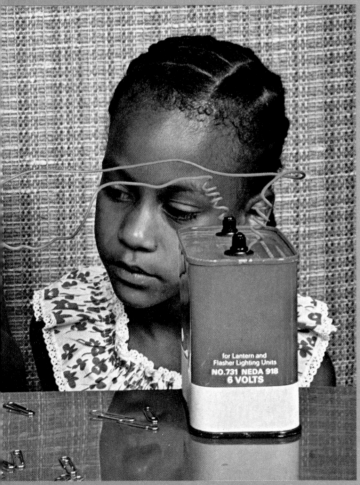

Now wrap a wire around
the nail.
Make electricity move
through the wire.
Now touch the nail to
the clips.
What happens?
Now stop the electricity
from moving.
What happens to the clips?

CHECKUP

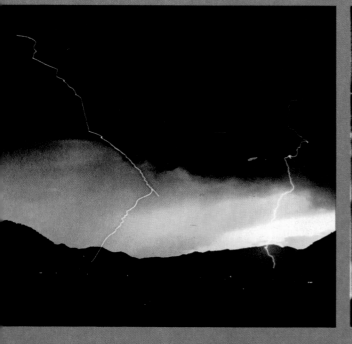

1. Which pictures show static electricity?
2. Which pictures show current electricity being used?
3. What kind of electricity collects on things?
4. What kind of electricity moves along a path?
5. What will stop electricity from moving?
6. What makes a path for electricity?
7. Find something that makes electricity.
8. How do we use electricity?

7

LEARNING ABOUT HEAT AND LIGHT

Heat and light are kinds of energy.

Where do you see light here?

Where do you think there is heat?

Where there is light, there is almost
   always heat.

Is there always light when there is heat?

How do you know when there is light?

How do you know when there is heat?

What kinds of energy do these pictures show?

Why does the cat like to sleep in the
   window?

What would you see if you were in these
   places?

What would you feel in these two places?

Why is the sun important to us?

How do you know how hot or cold it is?

How does a thermometer help us?

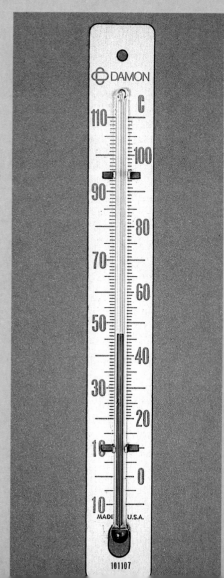

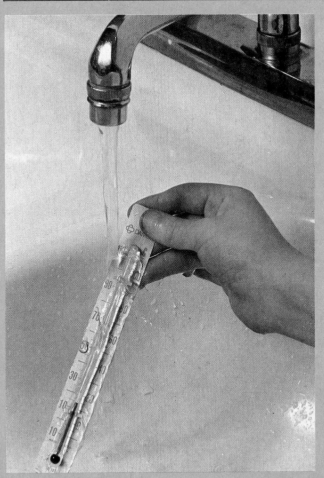

Have you ever played outside on a cold day?

It feels good to get inside.

How does heat get from the fire to the people?

Does heat move through water?

Does heat move through solids?

Look at the pictures on the next page.

How do they help you answer the questions?

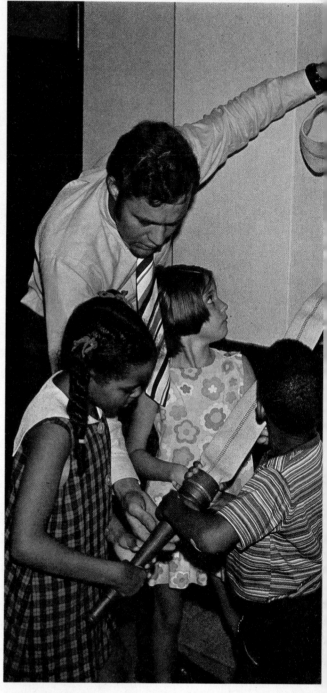

Fire gives off heat energy.

What else does it give off?

Fire can help us.

But fire can also hurt us.

Have you ever seen a fire like this?

How do you think it started?

How can we keep fires from
    starting?

Where have you seen things like these?

What are they used for?

Find some of these around your school.

What should you do if there is a fire?

What things shown here give off light?
Do they also give off heat?
What other things give off both light and heat?

Make a bulletin board like this one.
Find pictures of things that give off light.
Find pictures of things that give off heat.
Which things give off both heat and light?
Put your pictures in the right places.

Light comes from many things.
Where does most light come from in
   the day?
Where does light come from at night?
Which kind of light is brighter?

Some lights are very bright.
They can hurt your eyes.
We should not look at very
   bright lights.

Light helps you see things.

The light from things comes to your eyes.

Some things give off their own light.

Some things do not give off their own light.

They reflect light to your eyes.

Which things shown here give off light?

Which things shown here reflect light?

ACTIVITY

Which of these give off light?
Which of these reflect light?
Get some of these things.
Place them on a table in your classroom.
Talk to your classmates about them.

Many things reflect light.
Some things reflect light better than others.
Where is light reflected in the pictures?
Where else have you seen light reflected?
What kinds of things reflect light?
What kinds of things do not reflect light?

ACTIVITY

Get some things like these.
Then get a bright flashlight.
Go into a dark room.
Shine the light on each thing.
Which things reflect much light?
Which do not reflect much light?

ACTIVITY

Find out more about reflection.
Try these activities.
Draw a picture while
   looking in the mirror.
Is it hard, or easy?
Why?

Put two small mirrors together.
Do what the child is doing.
How many pennies do you see?
How many do you really have?

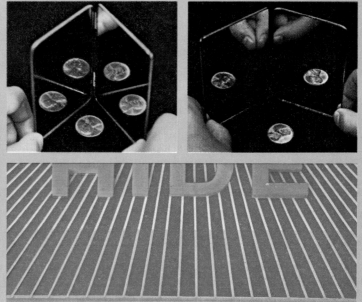

Hold a mirror along these letters.
What do you see?
Make some other letters like these.

ACTIVITY

Get some things of different colors.

Put them in a large paper bag.

Look into the bag but keep the light out.

What colors do you see in the bag?

Let more light into the bag.

Look in again.

Now what colors do you see?

What colors reflect the most light?

What colors do not reflect much light?

ACTIVITY

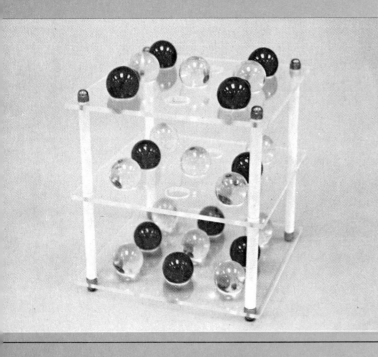

Light goes through some kinds of matter.

Light does not go through other kinds of matter.

Can you see through some kinds of matter?

Find each kind of matter in these pictures.

Find some things like these.
Test them with light.
Which ones will light go through?
Which can you see through?
Which do not let light go through?

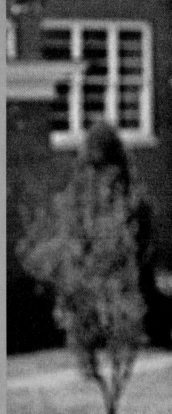

1. What kind of energy can you see?
2. What kind of energy can you feel?
3. How can you tell how hot or cold matter is?
4. Where does most of our light come from?
5. Name some things that give off their own light.
6. What kinds of things reflect light?
7. What kinds of things can you see through?
8. Name some things that give off heat and light.
9. What are some safe ways to use fire?
10. What should you do if a fire starts?

8

YOU AND PLANTS AND ANIMALS

What is a living thing?

What kinds of living things can you name?

How are all living things alike?

How are plants different from animals?

You know that you are a living thing.

Are you more like a plant, or an animal?

Why do you think so?

How does this dog walk most of the time?

What other animals walk on four legs?

How do you walk?

What other animals walk on two legs?
How are you like the dog?

In what ways are you different?

What parts of your body help you stand?

What parts of your body help you walk?

What other animals can walk like this?

Play follow-the-leader.

Have the leader pretend to be an animal.

Have the leader be a person.

How are you different when you are a person?

Does the boy see the crab?
Does the crab see the boy?
Can the crab think like the boy can?
Your brain helps you think.
What else does you brain help you do?

What is each of these living things doing?
Can you smell and hear?
Can you smell as well as the dog?
Can you hear as well as the rabbit?
Can any other animals read and write?

ACTIVITY

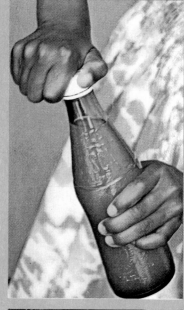

Look at all these pictures carefully.

What are the children doing?

Can any other animal do these things?

You can do them because you have a thumb.

Try to do these things without using your thumb.

Try to write your name without using your thumb.

How does your thumb help you?

Suppose you could not use your thumbs.

How would your life be different?

What are these children eating?
How does this food help them?
Where did the food come from?

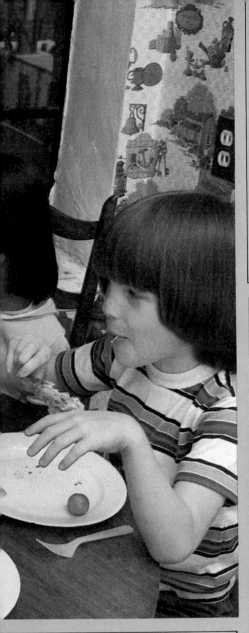

What kinds of foods do you see here?
Which of the foods do you like?
What other foods do you like?
Find out where the foods come from.

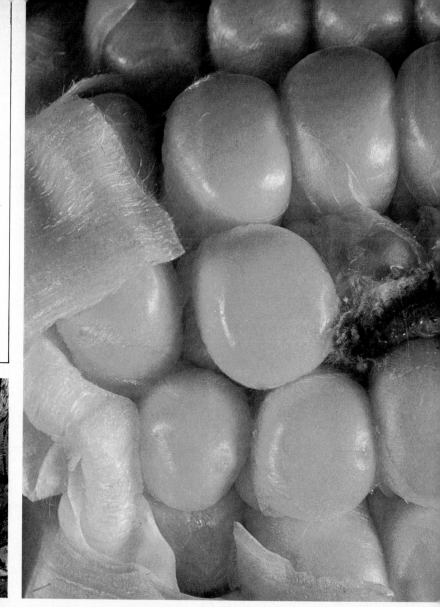

162

Mold is a tiny plant.

Mold grows on some foods that you eat.

Where is mold growing here?

Moldy foods can make you sick.

How can we keep mold from growing on our food?

ACTIVITY

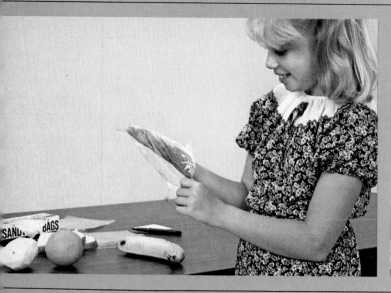 

Try to grow some mold.

You must give it food and water.

Put some food in plastic bags.

Put some bags in the light.

Put some bags in a warm, dark place.

Put other bags in the refrigerator.

Look at them every day.
Does mold grow on any
of the food?
What did you learn from
doing this?

Banana bread

Orange

Potato

You learned that tiny plants grow on food.

But the plants do not grow fast on cold food.

What is this boy doing?

How will it help protect the food?

Some animals eat the food that we grow.

What is this person doing?

How will this protect the food?

Some tiny plants and animals get into our bodies.

They use the energy we need.

They can make us sick.

The doctor can help protect you from getting sick.

What is the doctor doing to this boy?

How will this help him from getting sick?

1. How do you know you are a living thing?

2. What are some other living things?

3. How are you like plants and other animals?

4. How are you different from plants and other animals?

5. What do all living things need to stay alive?

6. What plants and animals do you use for food?

7. What plants and animals use our food?

8. What things can make you sick?

9. How can you keep yourself from getting sick?

GLOSSARY

attracts Pulls to or toward. A magnet pulls other metals toward itself.

battery An instrument that contains stored energy. The energy can be made into electricity.

current electricity Electricity that moves along a path.

desert A very dry region.

food web A term that describes how animals and plants depend on one another for food.

fresh water Water that is not too salty to drink.

gas Matter that has no shape. Air is a gas.

hibernate To pass the winter in a kind of sleep.

liquid Matter that flows. Water is a liquid.

lungs The breathing organs of certain air-breathing animals.

magnet A piece of metal that attracts other metals.

matter Anything that has weight and takes up space.

migrate To move to another place to find food. Animals usually migrate when the weather changes.

mirror A smooth object that reflects images.

mold A tiny plant that lives on other plants. Mold does not make its own food.

oceans Large bodies of salt water. The water in oceans is too salty to drink.

poles The ends of a magnet.

reflect To bounce back. Sound and light can bounce back from objects.

salt water Water that has salt in it. Ocean water is salt water.

shell A hard covering that protects an animal.

snail An animal with a soft body and a shell. Snails move very slowly.

solid Matter that does not flow. Metals are solids.

static electricity Electricity that collects on things and then jumps to other things.

switch Something that breaks or closes the path along which electricity moves.

temperature The degree of hotness or coldness. Temperature is measured by a thermometer.

thermometer An instrument that tells how hot or cold matter is.

tracks The prints left by animals when they move.

water vapor Water that has changed from a liquid to a gas.

weather Condition of the atmosphere over a certain region at any one time.

INDEX